A Poetry Unit

Take A Bite Out Of Rhyme

HAIKU

TANKA

ACROSTIC

LANTERN

SONNET

LIMERICK

COUPLET

DIAMONTE

CLERIHEW

QUATRAIN

STAIR POEM

CINQUAIN

CONCRETE

METAPHOR

SIMILE

Written by
Cindi Nolen Allen, Ph.D.

Illustrated by
Karen Neulinger

Educational
Impressions

For Dr. Dormalee Lindberg

ISBN 0-910857-62-8

EDUCATIONAL IMPRESSIONS, INC.
Hawthorne, NJ 07507

Table of Contents

To the Teacher

Take a Bite Out of Rhyme is a language arts activity book designed to expose learners to a variety of poetic devices and forms. A food theme prevails throughout as a tempting tool for promoting literary fun, fostering an interest in poetry, providing a sensory subject to write about, and sharing of common experiences.

When using *Take a Bite Out of Rhyme*, read the poetry examples aloud to your students. Have them observe both visual and auditory patterns that occur. Discuss the student activities that follow each example so that the purpose of each is clear. I find it more conducive to creative thinking processes if students do not have to worry about spelling errors. I encourage mine to spell phonetically and channel their energies toward the creation of ideas and the application of the various poetic forms. As a follow-up to each activity, I always allow ample time for my students to share and discuss their poetry.

Upon completion of *Take a Bite Out of Rhyme*, students can rewrite their poems, correcting any errors in spelling, and compile them into illustrated poetry books. Shape books lend themselves nicely to the food theme. My students enjoy holding authors' teas. We arrange to use the school library and then design and send invitations to parents, telling them of the day, place, and time. During the reception, parents are greeted at the door by some of the students. Other students are stationed around the room to give information about the project or to serve refreshments. The poetry books are displayed on library tables and an "About the Author" card, which includes a wallet sized photo of the child, is placed with each student's book.

Cindi Nolen Allen

COUPLETS

Couplets are two-lined poems with a fun and simple rhyming pattern. Each line has the same meter and their endings rhyme with one another. Humor is often used in couplets.

The following are examples of couplets:

A heap of macaroni filled the plate
Until my brother ate and ate and ate.

The wondrous smell of taffy filled the air
As my nose helped me find it at the fair.

Most people love baked beans and ham,
But mine are in the garbage can.

COUPLETS

Create a couplet about something you like to eat.

_____

_____

_____

Now create a couplet about something you dislike to eat.

_____

_____

_____

Illustrate one of your couplets in the box below.

QUATRAINS

This type of poetry always has four lines and rhymes in one of four ways. Poets use letters to show the pattern of rhyme. The four types of rhyme for a quatrain are: AABB, ABAB, ABBA, and ABCB.

(Analyze the patterns of rhyme of the following poems.)

French Fries

Golden brown French fries _____
Long, crispy and tender. _____
What a sight for hungry eyes _____
When on my plate for dinner. _____

Peanut Butter

Peanut butter, oh how handy! _____
Lunch box sandwiches quite dandy. _____
Add your favorite kind of jelly, _____
Then gobble up and send to belly. _____

Popcorn

Popcorn popping _____
On the stove in a pan. _____
I hardly think I can _____
Eat without stopping. _____

Gingerbread Man

The gingerbread man lay alone _____
In the oven baking. _____
Until the timer rang out loud _____
To signal time for taking. _____

QUATRAINS

Write four quatrains using the rhyming patterns shown on the right.

Tacos

_____ (A)

_____ (A)

_____ (B)

_____ (B)

Potato Chips

_____ (A)

_____ (B)

_____ (A)

_____ (B)

Soup

_____ (A)

_____ (B)

_____ (B)

_____ (A)

_____ (your choice)

_____ (A)

_____ (B)

_____ (C)

_____ (B)

9

ACROSTICS

An acrostic poem is one in which the name of a person, place or thing is written in a vertical (up-and-down) line. The poem is developed from the beginning letter on each line.

Chocolate

C hocolate is so yummy to eat.
H aving it is a special treat.
O ne little bite of a Hershey's Kiss
C an put me in a state of bliss.
O r
L icking a frozen chocolate bar
A s I take a summer ride in a car.
T otal pleasure is a chocolate treat.
E agerly I wait for chocolate to eat!

ACROSTICS

Brainstorm some food words you could use to write an acrostic poem.

_____   _____

_____   _____

_____   _____

_____   _____

_____   _____

Choose one of your favorite ideas from above. Use it to write an acrostic poem. Make the first letter in each line darker than the others.

CONCRETE POEMS

Concrete poetry is written in the shape of the topic of the poem. Rhyme is not important in concrete poetry. Look at the poems below and observe both their visual and written components. One poem uses only descriptive words, while the other poem gives a thought about the topic.

PICKLE

Green, crunchy, juicy, sliced, whole, sour pickle.

KISS

A silvery wrapper holds this chocolate treat for me to eat.

CONCRETE POEMS

Think of a food you like to eat. _____

List many different words that describe your food or that tell how you feel about it.

_____   _____   _____

_____   _____   _____

_____   _____   _____

_____   _____   _____

Use what you wrote to help you create a concrete poem in the space below.

_____ (Title)

13

HAIKU

Haiku is a Japanese poem with no rhyme. Haiku poems have only three lines, each with a certain number of syllables.

Here is the pattern:

    line 1 = 5 syllables

    line 2 = 7 syllables

    line 3 = 5 syllables

(Count the number of syllables in each line.)

Apples

Apples round and red _____

Hanging from full, green branches _____

Waiting to be picked. _____

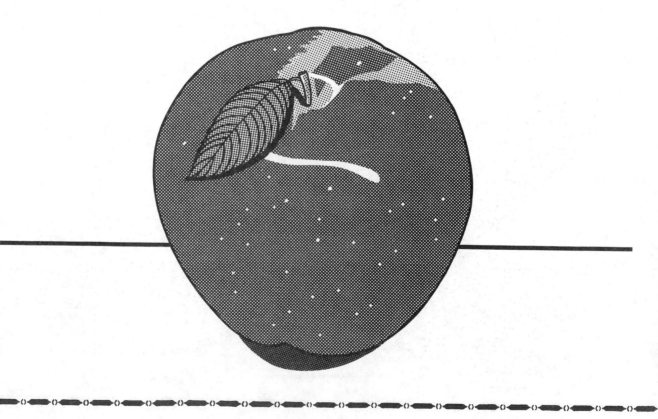

HAIKU

Haiku is often used to write about something in nature. Write two haiku poems. Use a fruit as the topic for one and a vegetable for the topic of the other.

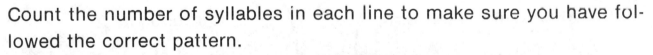

_____

_____ _____

_____ _____

_____

_____ _____

_____ _____

_____

Count the number of syllables in each line to make sure you have followed the correct pattern.

LANTERN POEMS

Lantern poems are written in the shape of Japanese lanterns. Their shape is formed by using five lines, each with a different number of syllables. The number of syllables for each line are:

line 1 = 1 syllable

line 2 = 2 syllables

line 3 = 3 syllables

line 4 = 4 syllables

line 5 = 1 syllable

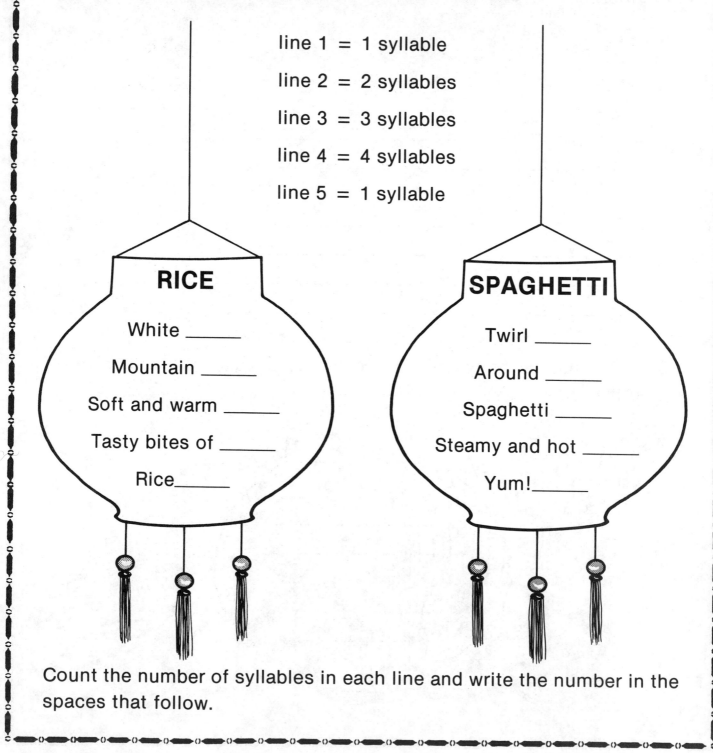

RICE

White _____

Mountain _____

Soft and warm _____

Tasty bites of _____

Rice _____

SPAGHETTI

Twirl _____

Around _____

Spaghetti _____

Steamy and hot _____

Yum! _____

Count the number of syllables in each line and write the number in the spaces that follow.

LANTERN POEMS

Create two lantern poems using ideas from the following list:

hot dog	peas	pie
steak	corn	cake
fish	beets	cookies

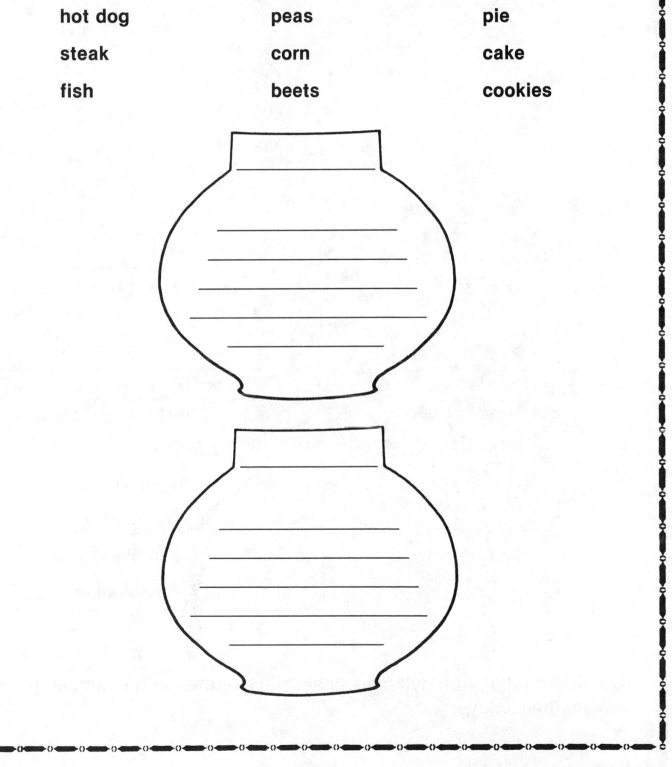

TANKA

Tanka is another form of Japanese poetry that depends on the number of lines and syllables instead of rhyme. This is the pattern:

line 1 = 5 syllables

line 2 = 7 syllables

line 3 = 5 syllables

line 4 = 7 syllables

line 5 = 7 syllables

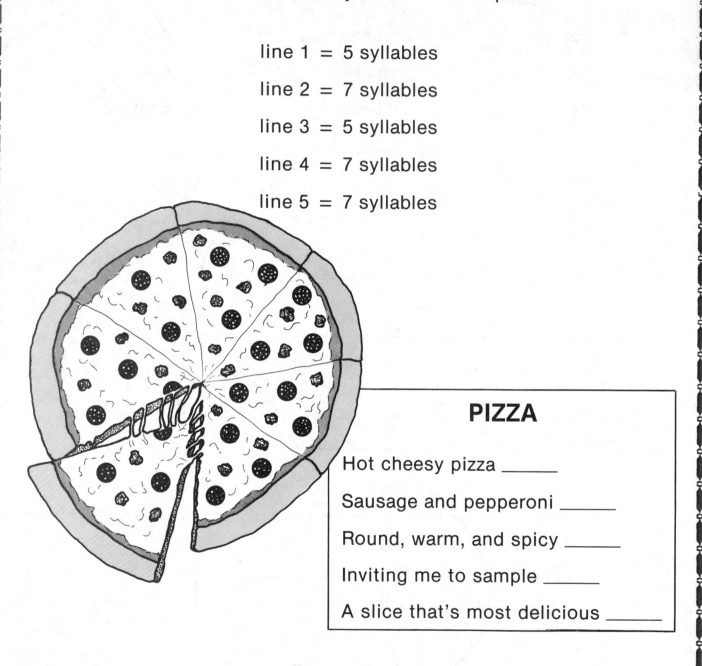

PIZZA

Hot cheesy pizza _____

Sausage and pepperoni _____

Round, warm, and spicy _____

Inviting me to sample _____

A slice that's most delicious _____

Count the number of syllables in each line and write the number in the spaces that follow.

TANKA

Think of one of your favorite foods and write a Tanka poem about it. Make sure you follow the pattern by using the correct number of syllables.

_____

_____ _____

_____ _____

_____ _____

_____ _____

_____ _____

Count the number of syllables in each line of your Tanka and write the numbers in the spaces following the lines.

Use a colored pencil or marker to make a line between each syllable in your poem.

Illustrate your poem.

CINQUAINS

Cinquain is a form of poetry that has a total of five lines. The lines depend on parts of speech and syllables rather than rhyme. The pattern for a cinquain is:

line 1 = One noun of 2 syllables

line 2 = Adjective(s) with a total of 4 syllables that describe the noun

line 3 = Words showing action and having a total of 6 syllables (-ing words work well)

line 4 = Words with a total of 8 syllables that tell how you feel about the noun

line 5 = Another noun of 2 syllables that makes you think of the first noun

CHERRIES

Cherries _____

Juicy, round, red _____

Picking, tasting, eating _____

A tasty treat at any time _____

Ruby _____

Count the number of syllables in each line and write the number in the spaces that follow.

CINQUAINS

Write a cinquain poem about lemons.

LEMONS

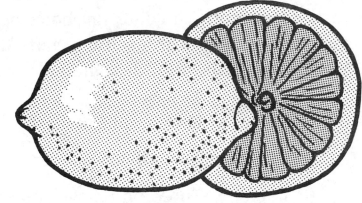

_____ _____

_____ _____

_____ _____

_____ _____

_____ _____

Write a cinquain poem about jello.

JELLO

_____ _____

_____ _____

_____ _____

_____ _____

_____ _____

Count the number of syllables in each line of your poems and write the numbers in the spaces following the lines.

Have a friend check your poems for the correct parts of speech.

DIAMONTES

Diamonte poems are diamond-shaped poems that are written using parts of speech. They are fun because the top half of the diamond is very different from the bottom half. The poem has seven lines in all. Here is the pattern for a diamonte:

line 1 = One noun (#1)

line 2 = Two adjectives describing noun #1

line 3 = Three participles that end in -ing and tell about noun #1

line 4 = Four more nouns: the first two are related to noun #1 and the second two are related to noun #2

line 5 = Three participles that end in -ing and tell about noun #2

line 6 = Two adjectives that describe noun #2

line 7 = One noun (#2)

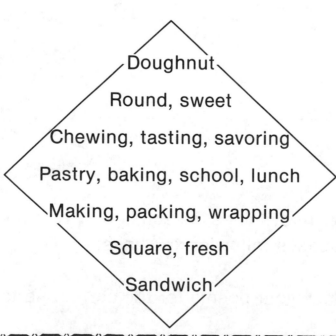

Doughnut
Round, sweet
Chewing, tasting, savoring
Pastry, baking, school, lunch
Making, packing, wrapping
Square, fresh
Sandwich

DIAMONTES

Think of pairs of foods that are opposites and could be used to write a diamonte poem. Write the pairs below.

Example: doughnut / sandwich

_____ / _____

_____ / _____

_____ / _____

_____ / _____

_____ / _____

_____ / _____

Create a diamonte using ideas about one of the pairs from above.

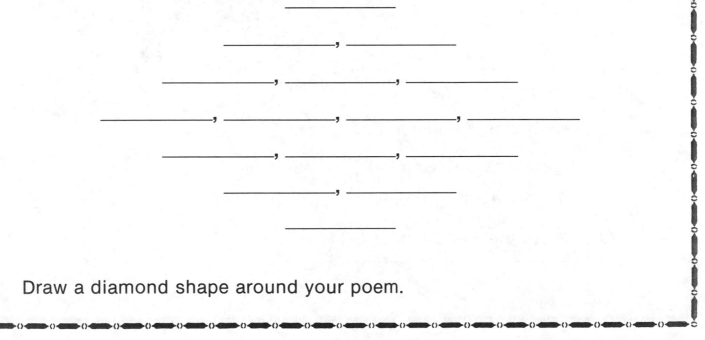

_____

_____ , _____

_____ , _____ , _____

_____ , _____ , _____ , _____

_____ , _____ , _____

_____ , _____

_____

Draw a diamond shape around your poem.

LIMERICKS

A limerick is a whimsical poem with only five lines. This type of poem depends on rhythm and rhyme. Lines one, two and five rhyme with each other. Lines three and four rhyme with each other. (AABBA) Lines one, two, and five have three rhythmic parts, or feet. Lines three and four are shorter and contain only two feet; they are indented. Each foot in a limerick contains one or two unstressed syllables followed by a stressed syllable.

Look at the poem below and mark each syllable as either stressed (–) or unstressed (ᴗ). Then draw a line between each foot in the poem. The first line has been done for you.

Ă děssērt/Ĭ ăttēmptĕd tŏ māke;

The result was an upside down cake.

    I gave some to a friend,

    Who said, "Blah!" at the end

And asked me to no longer bake!

LIMERICKS

Write a limerick that has a food theme.

_____

_____

_____

_____

_____

Design an illustration for your limerick.

SONNETS

A sonnet is a poem of fourteen lines. It begins with three quatrains and ends with one couplet. Read the following sonnet.

DECISIONS

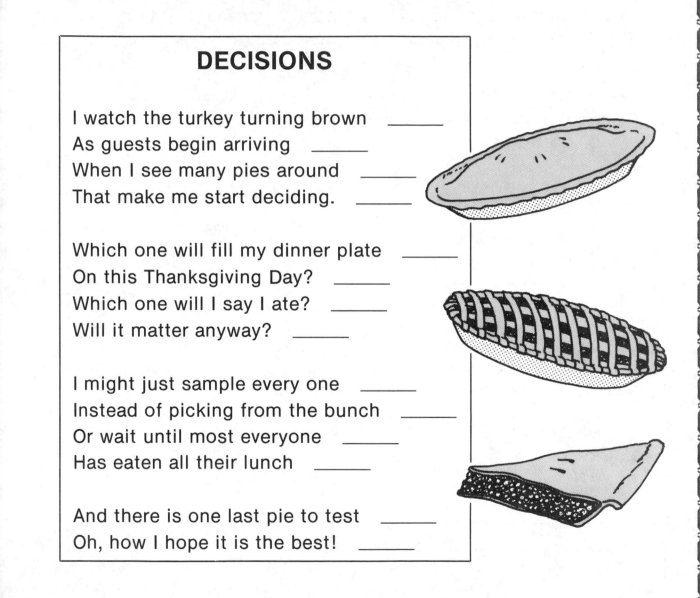

I watch the turkey turning brown _____
As guests begin arriving _____
When I see many pies around _____
That make me start deciding. _____

Which one will fill my dinner plate _____
On this Thanksgiving Day? _____
Which one will I say I ate? _____
Will it matter anyway? _____

I might just sample every one _____
Instead of picking from the bunch _____
Or wait until most everyone _____
Has eaten all their lunch _____

And there is one last pie to test _____
Oh, how I hope it is the best! _____

Use capital letters to mark the rhyming patterns of the quatrains and the couplet.

Using the symbols for stressed (−) and unstressed (u) syllables, analyze each of the fourteen lines in "Decisions." Mark (/) each foot.

SONNETS

Creating a sonnet is not as hard as it looks. Follow the steps below to create your own sonnet with a food theme. First, think of some foods you might want to write about. Next, concentrate on writing down your ideas about the food. Don't try to plan ahead too far. Work on one quatrain at a time. Make sure you use the same rhyming pattern for all three quatrains. When the quatrains are finished, complete the poem with a couplet. Don't forget to title your poem!

_____

1st quatrain
_____
_____
_____
_____

2nd quatrain
_____
_____
_____
_____

3rd quatrain
_____
_____
_____
_____

4th quatrain
_____
_____
_____
_____

couplet
_____
_____

DIFFERENT FEET
FOR A DIFFERENT BEAT

**There are five kinds of poetic feet.
Each one having a different beat.**

An **iambic foot** contains one unstressed syllable followed by one stressed syllable.

A **trochee foot** has one stressed syllable followed by one unstressed syllable.

A **dactyl foot** contains one stressed syllable followed by two unstressed syllables.

An **anapest foot** is a dactyl in reverse. It has two unstressed syllables followed by one stressed syllable.

A **spondee foot** has two accented syllables.

Which of the poetic feet are used in the couplet at the beginning of this page? _____

How many feet are in each line? _____
Draw a line between each foot.

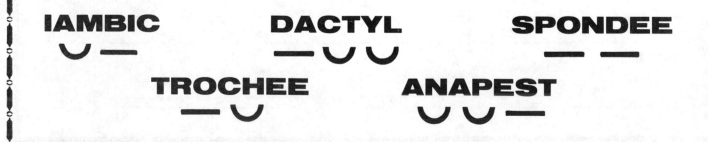

DIFFERENT FEET
FOR A DIFFERENT BEAT

Each of the following sentences shows an example of a different type of poetic foot. Read them and mark each syllable with the symbol for stressed (−) or unstressed (υ). Count the number of feet in each line. Read them aloud with the appropriate rhythm.

IAMBIC FOOT

I ate a pie last night.
My stomach is a sight.

How many feet in each line? _____

TROCHEE FOOT

Ice cream, taffy, malteds, candy.
Peanuts, pretzels—it's all dandy!

How many feet in each line? _____

DACTYL FOOT

Some are red, some are green.
I don't like any bean.

How many feet in each line? _____

ANAPEST FOOT

Big bad John wants his cake
Or a mess he will make.

How many feet in each line? _____

SPONDEE FOOT

Mix, mix; add eggs and shake.
Blend well and bake your cake.

How many feet in each line? _____

CLERIHEWS

Clerihew is a funny poetic form which was created by an English writer named Edmund Clerihew Bentley. These poems have only four lines. Here are the rules:

line 1 = Must end with a person's name

line 2 = Rhymes with line 1

line 3 = Rhymes with line 4

line 4 = Rhymes with line 3

BIG JOE

Into the lunchroom walked **BIG JOE.**
He walked in tall, but he walked in slow.
Under each arm was a big lunch sack
And on his back was a lunch backpack.

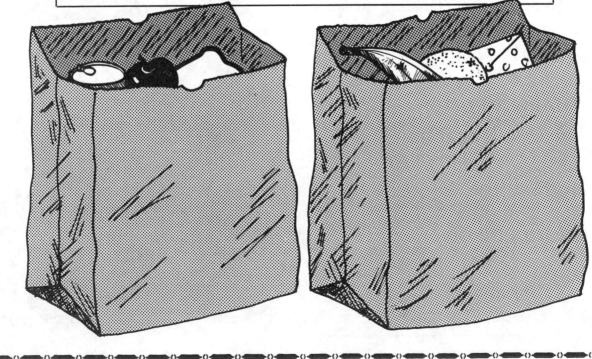

CLERIHEWS

The poem on the preceding page was about "Big Joe." Draw a picture showing what you think Big Joe would have for lunch.

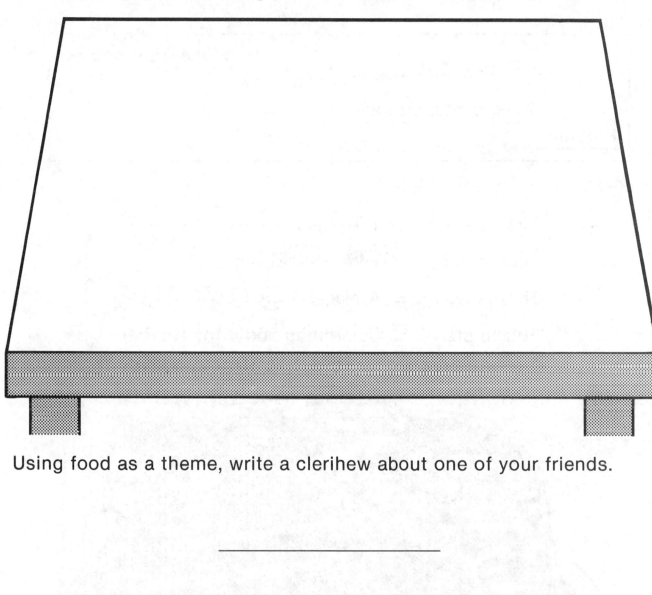

Using food as a theme, write a clerihew about one of your friends.

_____

_____

_____

_____

_____

STAIR POETRY

A poem can be written using stair steps as the visual form for building ideas about a topic. Look at the poem below.

Wonderful topping
On the cake
Pink, creamy, sweet
Frosting

First step	=	The topic
Second step	=	Three adjectives
Third step	=	A place or time
Fourth step	=	Something about the topic

STAIR POETRY

Write a stair poem about pancakes.

PANCAKES

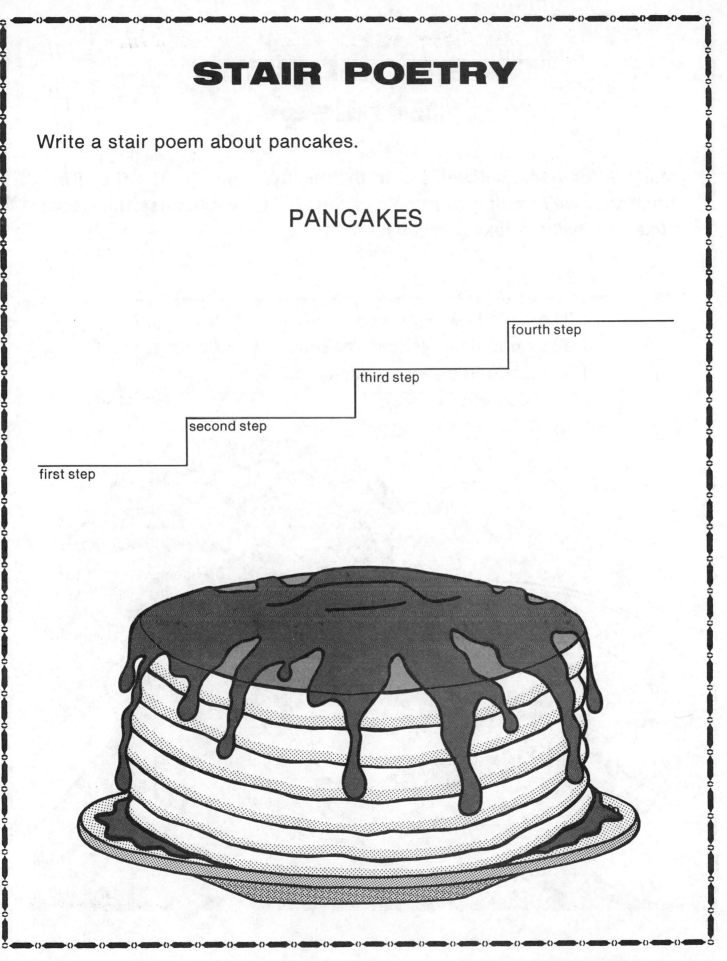

fourth step

third step

second step

first step

TASTY TIDBITS:
Similes

Many different techniques add to the quality of poetry. The first tasty tidbit that we're going to sample is the simile. Similes use the words "like" or "as" to make comparisons.

> The cake is **as** light **as** a feather.
> The chocolate melts **like** a brown river flowing.
> The soup is steaming **like** an active volcano.

SIMILES

Write some similes of your own.
Use food as the theme.

1. _____

2. _____

3. _____

4. _____

5. _____

Illustrate one of your similes.

35

TASTY TIDBITS:
Metaphors

Metaphors, like similes, make comparisons; however, metaphors make the comparisons without using the words "like" or "as."

Observe the comparisons in the sentences below.

> The **pudding** is a velvet **cream**.
> The **potatoes** are a fluffy **mountain**.
> The **strawberry** is a brilliant **jewel**.

METAPHORS

Try writing your own metaphors about food. Remember **not** to use "like" or "as."

1. _____

2. _____

3. _____

4. _____

5. _____

6. _____

7. _____

8. _____

9. _____

10. _____

Illustrate one of your metaphors.

TASTY TIDBITS:
Onomatopoeia

Onomatopoeia uses words whose sounds give suggestions to your senses. In other words, the word makes you think of the action.

> The steak **sizzled.**
> **She crunched** the candy.
> He **slurped** up the soup.

Write some words that have an onomatopoetic sound.

_____   _____

_____   _____

_____   _____

_____   _____

_____   _____

ONOMATOPOEIA

Use some of the words to write sentences that use onomatopoeia.
Remember to write about food.

1. _____

2. _____

3. _____

4. _____

5. _____

Illustrate one of your sentences.

MORE TASTY TIDBITS:
Alliteration and Assonance

ALLITERATION

Alliteration repeats the same beginning sound in two or more neighboring words to create a special effect. The following sentences contain examples of alliteration:

Crispy **c**ookies **c**an **c**rumble.

Mushy **m**arshmallows **m**ake **m**esses for **M**om.

French **f**ries make **f**ine **f**inger **f**oods.

ASSONANCE

Assonance is the repetition of a vowel sound. Note the repetition of the short "o" sound in the following sentence:

H**o**t d**o**gs are **o**ften **o**ffered at b**a**ll games.

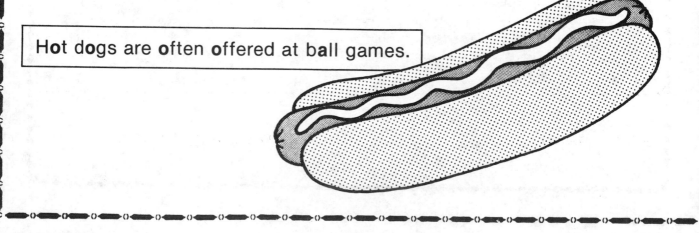

ALLITERATION
AND
ASSONANCE

Using food as the theme, write some sentences using alliteration.

1. _____

2. _____

3. _____

4. _____

5. _____

Create a couplet about food that uses alliteration.

_____

_____

Now create your own sentences about food using assonance.

1. _____

2. _____

3. _____

4. _____

5. _____

Identify the vowel sound you are repeating in each sentence.

1. _____   2. _____   3. _____   4. _____   5. _____

41

MIX AND MATCH

Pick a food-related special occasion. Brainstorm several food or food-related words. Using as many words as possible, arrange one at the beginning of each line. Match each with a thought which completes a phrase or sentence for each line. Your finished product will be a free form poem. Give your poem a title.

EXAMPLE:

chocolate	cake	frosting
white	candles	Happy Birthday
flames		

THE BIRTHDAY

Cake	a special treat of
Chocolate	brown and yummy.
Frosting	spread in thick
White	mounds.
"Happy Birthday!"	written in blue ice.
Candles	burning with
Flames	that announce another year.

MIX AND MATCH

Following the directions on the previous page, create your own free form poem about a food-related special occasion.

Brainstorm:

_____   _____   _____

_____   _____   _____

_____   _____   _____

_____

_____   _____

_____   _____

_____   _____

_____   _____

_____   _____

_____   _____

STRIKE UP THE BAND!

Create a poem about food which is to be sung to the tune of "Twinkle, Twinkle, Little Star." Write at least two verses, each with three couplets.

_____

_____

_____

_____

_____

_____

_____

_____

_____

_____

_____

_____

_____

POSTER POETRY

Design a poster to promote poetry.

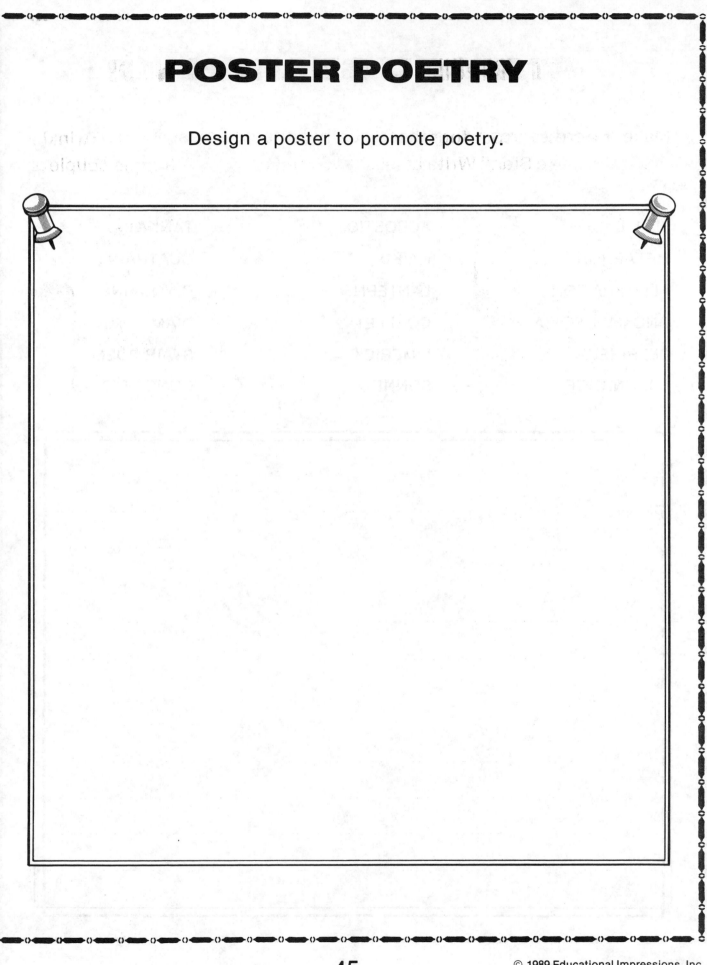

WORD SEARCH

Make a word search using these poetry pattern names.

SIMILE	ACROSTIC	TANKA
METAPHOR	HAIKU	QUATRAIN
ALLITERATION	LANTERN	CINQUAIN
ONOMATOPOEIA	COUPLET	DIAMONTE
CLERIHEW	LIMERICK	STAIR POEM
ASSONANCE	SONNET	CONCRETE

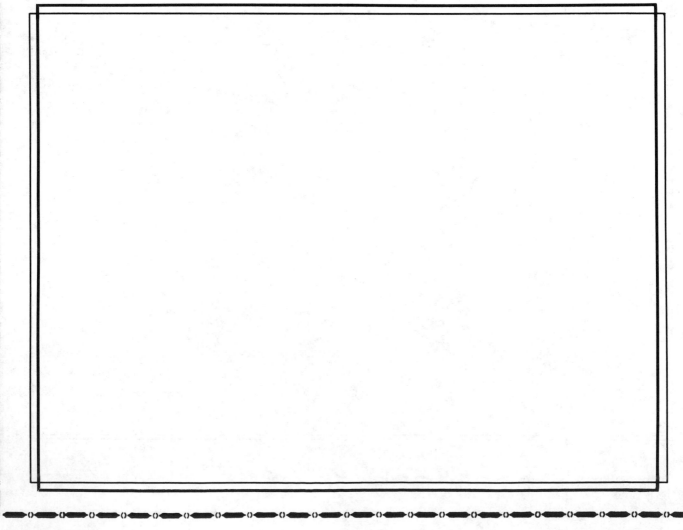

TAKE A BITE OUT OF RHYME

QUATRAIN

CONCRETE

TANKA

HAIKU

COUPLET

SONNET

METAPHOR

STAIR POEM

CINQUAIN

ACROSTIC

LANTERN

LIMERICK

SIMILE

CLERIHEW

DIAMONTE

PIÈCE DE RÉSISTANCE

Compile your poetry creations into an illustrated book:

1. Correct all spelling and punctuation errors on the poems you have written.
2. Invent a title for your book.
3. Design a cover. You might like to make your book the shape of one of your favorite foods.
4. Include two pages for each poem: one for the poem and one for the illustration that goes with it.
5. Rewrite the corrected poems on every other book page.
6. Create an illustration to go with each poem on the blank page beside it.
7. Make a title page.
8. Make a dedication page.
9. Make a Table of Contents. It would be helpful to label each kind of poem.
10. Bind your book pages and cover together.

Organize an author's tea:

1. Decide on a day, time, and place.
2. Create invitations for parents and other guests.
3. Plan what refreshments to serve.
4. Choose some music to play while guests are arriving.
5. Decide who will greet guests at the door, who will serve refreshments, and who will answer questions that guests may have.
6. Plan ahead for the way in which the books will be displayed.
7. Make an "About the Author" card for each student and display it with each book.
8. Allow some time for guests to browse through the books.
9. Provide seating for the guests.
10. Take turns reading the books (or selections from the books) as the guests enjoy the refreshments.